A KINTSUGI PARABLE

Angie Clark

For Ashton,
because it's not only rulers that are broken
when living a broken-ruler life.

CONTENTS

FOREWORD   i

PREFACE   v

PARABLE   vii

PART 1: BROKENNESS   **1**

AFTER THE FIRE   **1**

A Life of Surrender   3

The Mission   6

Once Upon a Ceramics Shop   8

BROKEN   **9**

Broken Things in Scripture   12

When the Potter Allows the Breaking   14

Careless Handlers   16

Malicious Breaks   19

BROKEN OR SHATTERED   **22**

THE REPAIR PROCESS   **23**

Keeping Hope Alive   25

We Can't Fix Ourselves   29

Giving God All the Pieces   30

PART 2: FILLED   **33**

KINTSUGI REPAIR   **33**

Repair Type 1: Hibi - Filled   33

Repair Type 2: Kake No Kintsugi Re - Missing Piece   37

Bitterness   42

PART 3: CALLED   **47**

Repair Type 3: Yobitsugi – Call   47

HIS POWER THROUGH MY WEAKNESS   **51**

PART 4: TOGETHER FOREVER 53

SAFE 53
TOGETHER 56
FOREVER 58

ACKNOWLEDGEMENTS 61

SMALL GROUP ADAPTATION 63

Week 1: Brokenness 63
Week 2: Repair types 1 & 2 (Filled) 63
Week 3: Repair type 3 (Called) 64
Week 4: Together Forever 65

FOREWORD

I like to throw things away. Yes, I said it. Whether it's chipped or cracked, stained or torn, expired or inefficient, it's time to say goodbye. Some call it a gift, others a curse, but this habit has been part of my personality since childhood. When my dog chewed off the foot of my favorite Barbie or when I dripped huckleberry ice cream on my white Sunday dress, those items quickly lost their value in my mind; their presence among my non-crippled Barbies and clean, stainless clothes screamed loudly of imperfection. After I grieved them, I buried them delicately in the garbage can or garage-sale box, along with the joy they had once brought me. Then, and only then, I would sigh with relief. My world was back in order.

Fast forward to my teenage years and my knack for eliminating items became a full-blown skill. In fact, no food was safe in our home. My family members would hide leftovers in the fridge for fear that I would see them, and like a judge without a jury, sentence those perishables to a dark cell. Once, as a kind of therapeutic exercise, I began an episode of *Hoarders*. That's the end of the story. I only made it through ten minutes before the anxiety became unbearable. (I could not crawl out of that nightmare fast enough.) To this day, when the church storage room needs to be purged and organized, there I am with garbage cans and clear plastic bins to the rescue.

i

But as I hurried into adulthood with my tidied résumé and seemingly-perfect life, I began to notice the shadow side of my personality. There were parts of my story that I could not cut out, throw away, or cover up. I could not erase my past mistakes or disappointments. What now? I felt my own life decreasing in value, and I couldn't remove the cracks without throwing away the entire vessel. So, I did what most people do. I hid those less-than-Insta-glamorous parts of my life in the back of the cabinet, where most chipped, but still useable, cups go.

I recall purchasing the book, *The Me I Want to Be*, by John Ortberg during Bible school, hoping I could someday be that perfect version of myself that God intended. With all my might and determination, I could not accomplish what only the Master Potter could do in my life.

I finally broke. I mean *really* broke. After spending years in a serious relationship, I felt shattered with the guilt of a wasted season, knowing there was a piece of my life I could never get back. If my pieces had not landed at the feet of Jesus, I'm afraid to think of what I would have thrown away.

Enter my friend: Angie Clark.

I met Angie at a pivotal point in my healing process. I was beginning to see the light break amid the dark clouds of a disappointed dream. I was feeling hope for a new life in Christ. Yes, I was broken, but somehow – through God's grace – I felt I could be made whole. I could be "the me *God* wants me to be" and not my own idea of perfection. I wasn't sure how that would ever happen, but God knew exactly what He was doing. He brought Angie into my life like a sweet, Hawaiian breeze. Angie smiled and saw me as someone whole, someone that God was working on. It was only a matter of time before I realized that Angie was part of that missing piece, someone God was using to bring restoration in my life.

That is the beauty of our Master Potter. When Angie asked me to write the foreword to this book on *kintsugi*, the ancient Japanese practice of repairing broken pottery, I thought this must be an elaborate joke. I am the antithesis of *kintsugi*. I am the thrower-away-of-things. And yet, somehow, I think the irony of it all makes the process of *kintsugi* and the story of my life in Christ all the more beautiful. I pray it does the same for you.

—Cori Lucas

PREFACE

I keep a polyhedral die, the one pictured above, in my desk drawer at the office as a reminder that no one angle, or opinion, covers an entire matter. When I feel locked into one way of thinking or can only see a situation from one side, it reminds me to reach out to ask for other perspectives from people I respect and trust. I may not adopt a differing viewpoint, but I value the perspective. I realize that because of our varied personality types, temperaments, life experiences and brain neurology, we all interpret the same types of events through very different lenses. This little book is a product of those encounters, and I trust will serve as a lens you can use when needed.

In the reading I've been doing over the past few years, and in the resulting conversations I've been having, there are a few common themes. They have to do with being vulnerable and authentic. I will be the first to admit how painfully aware I am of my own shortcomings and brokenness, and how I don't necessarily relish people gawking at my scars. I also acknowledge how much my weaknesses would like to muzzle the testimony of how God is at work in the broken parts of my life, but I choose not to be silent. Through reflection over these past months, I have come to see my deficiencies, and perhaps character flaws, as opportunities in which God would like to display His power through me.

Enter the story of kintsugi, a type of Japanese pottery repair that is not only aesthetically pleasing but adds value to the original piece. The Japanese word, kintsugi (金継ぎ), means gold splice or golden joinery. Feel free to Google it. Some of the examples of kintsugi are quite something. Some examples today might include a small kintsugi antique on Ebay that costs hundreds of dollars. It's hard to believe a small teacup purchased for a few dollars, aged with time and repaired using the kintsugi technique, is worth exponentially more than its original sale price.

You may be jumping ahead of me right now. Go ahead. There's room in this world for your ideas and mine. The kintsugi parable has given me a way to share meaningful lessons I've learned about brokenness and being repaired by the Master Potter in a way that's hopefully easy to visualize and consider. The things I don't mention here leave room for your thoughts and insights, your stories and struggles. Please be sure to share them with others; they're too rich to keep to yourself.

And now, without further ado, the kintsugi parable.

PARABLE

As the bowl completed its last revolution around the Potter's wheel, the keen eye of the Potter saw that it was just as He had imagined it. Balanced, strong, and ready for the drying season where further shaping and trimming would occur. Although the bowl didn't see it coming, it was headed to a few rounds in the fire. Next, it would need sanding and potentially a little grinding away at rough spots where it's glorious glaze had touched the kiln. It was not to be an overnight transformation, but a steady march toward its destiny as a simple bowl of great service, marked by the Master Potter whose seal it would ultimately bear.

Emerging from that arduous creation process, the finished bowl began its life of service, enjoying all the washings, the polishing, the displaying of itself and the holding of things, acknowledging itself as a cherished and favored vessel. It seemed life would go on this way forever.

Over time, it witnessed the shattering of a neighboring bowl that had slipped from the table to the floor. It had even felt a shard of another vessel ping off its outer rim. Close ups and close calls, until one day, arising from the carelessness of a handler, the first of many hairline cracks appeared.

Imperfect? Yes. Ruined? No.

Still highly valued, it was treated with care.

Still usable, until the day it wasn't.

On that fateful day, it laid, helpless, broken in the hands of the Master Potter. Four pieces, only three of which could be found, disconnected from itself. Though not shattered, it was unable to put itself back together; once again it was completely at the mercy of the Master. Would it be discarded? Swept away? Left in pieces forever?

It was then that an unfamiliar scent filled the air. Some would call it a stench. But to a broken bowl as this one, it was a smell that brought hope. The Master had begun mixing the semi-poisonous resin with wheat flour, a sure sign that a repair was imminent. The pieces went back together with the resin-mixture, filling the gap of the missing piece. This bowl would be whole again.

Over the next several weeks of intensive care, the excess resin that had been used to put the bowl back together was ground away from the seams, and the black lacquer was applied to all the cracks and gaps fusing the resin and the original finish of the bowl together. It was then set to dry in a place of obscurity, warm and damp until the day it was taken out to the Potter's repair desk, where more grinding of the lacquer and meticulous smoothing ensued for what seemed an eternity.

That's when the proverbial light at the end of the tunnel appeared. Once the red lacquer for the sealing finish was squeezed out of a paper tube like thick blood, a fine thin brush was brought out. It was carefully dragged through the thick, red lacquer before beginning its journey, tracing the scars across the surface of the bowl. It was put away to dry again before being brought out to the Potter's repair table for what the bowl assumed was the final step in the process.

There was a light, tapping sound. Gold dust began to fall from a straw in the Potter's hand. As the gold fell, it was pulled deep into the red lacquer. Light, feathery touches tapped the gold down and brushed the excess away. Exhilarating! Almost there! More tapping. More gold dust. More gentle sweeps across the surface of the bowl. Such a relief!

When it was over, much to the bowl's surprise, the now gold-streaked vessel found itself not on display as it had expected, but back on the drying shelf. Alone again. Numb with disappointment.

It wasn't a long wait until the bowl was brought out one last time. It had no expectations now, but was simply at rest in the Potter's hands. That's when the burnishing began, coaxing the gold to shine by rubbing it into the lacquer and wiping any excess away. Sometimes the burnishing felt a lot like being rubbed the wrong way, but it brought the shine, which was the intent of the Master Potter.

Through the whole ordeal, the Potter patiently and caringly tended to the process. You see, He was committed to finishing what He began. Nothing He did was intended to destroy the bowl, as it was one of His creations. He was quite happy to save this one bowl, a masterpiece. He was aware that this kind of transformation alters the purpose of a vessel. In this case, the bowl was no longer a simple serving bowl, but it now existed as a highly valued heirloom, ultimately pointing all who saw it to admire the Master Potter for His skill and commitment.

As it added beauty to its surroundings, it would also bring the Master Potter business from others. This little *kintsugi* bowl existed now to make His name great.

PART 1: BROKENNESS

AFTER THE FIRE

After the fire is over
After the ashes cool
After the smoke has blown away
I will be here for you…

Slowly, Slowly
We turn the page of life
Growing, Knowing
It comes at quite a price
~Amy Grant, 2003

A friend that is there for me after the fire is the kind of friend I'm looking for. It's the kind of friend I aspire to be, because I know there is life after the fire – and that life is not intended to be lived alone.

For those of us living us jars of clay which contain a great treasure from above,[1] we know we can't spend our lives on the Potter's wheel nor in the firing kiln. We are each purposed with a usefulness designed to point to the Master Potter's creativity and incredible skill. Accepting our beauty, in addition to our functionality, is part of the process of serving well and fulfilling our purpose; denying that beauty makes the process agonizingly difficult.

For me, growing up as a Christian, I heard stories of the Potter and the clay from the Old Testament books of Isaiah and Jeremiah. My personal history made it easy for me to conclude that I was often the clay in the story that gave the Potter resistance, resulting in continuous forming from His hands. By drawing truth from the original story, and to keep myself from going in circles the rest of my life, I yielded fully to the Master Potter's pressure, so I could get down off His wheel and get on with whatever program God had for me.

I earned my degrees in Christian Education and Missions, surviving the fire multiple times before launching into a job that allowed me to really serve those around me. My experiences to that point confirmed that this world was quite a hazardous place for jars of clay, especially for ones such as myself. I'd made it through the fire, but unlike the famous Hebrew three, I'm pretty sure there was still a little smell of smoke on me.

Life is what comes after the fire, and as you may know, it's not all unicorns and rainbows. Navigating life requires surrender and trust in the One who commissioned you to be your full self exactly as He designed.

A LIFE OF SURRENDER

I can hear a Singaporean accent asking me, "Surrender wha ting?" My response in kind, "erry ting, la."

Everything! Control, finances, dreams, reputation—you name it. Just because one graduates from the wheel, doesn't mean surrender is optional in the life of service that follows. Surrender will get you off the wheel, and surrender will keep you from losing your mind when God's fairness is called into question.

Surrendering to God every little thing is a spiritual workout. It creates a kind of muscle memory that adds up over time and builds a two-way trust between you and God. He can trust you and you will have a track record set down for trusting Him. It's not blindly trusting someone who's unworthy of your story. Of all the people in your life, He is the worthiest of your trust and the most deserving of your surrender.

On the list of what I need to surrender is anything that doesn't equip, enhance, or nurture the purpose of my existence, which is the same as yours by the way: bringing glory to Jesus. My advice to myself when I'm grasping at things is, "Girl, don't hold too tightly to anything you value that clouds His stamp on you."

My grandpa used to wrestle, or wrassle, with my brother, cousins, and I every summer until we got too big for him to handle. It was like WWF smackdown family edition. He would put some serious moves on us, and I have at least one family photo to prove it. It was all in good fun, but he was serious about making us cry "UNCLE!" which was our code word for surrender, at least temporarily. I learned from him a little about knowing when to hold up, fold up, when to walk away, and when to run. He was also a pretty slick blackjack dealer, but that's a story for another time.

So yes, I am familiar with surrender. And as an Enneagram nine, it's something I now realize comes naturally to me and I do it on a regular basis. For example, if out of the blue you want me to select where we should eat lunch, it's probably not going to happen. Try to pick a fight with me over something that doesn't matter to me and you're on your own. With others, I often surrender what I want because I value what would make them happier. Part of this is because as a single adult, I make so many decisions on my own that it's nice to have someone else make a decision for me once in a while. And when I'm not in the mood or just can't bring myself to surrender, my solution is to withdraw so that I won't have to.

Funny thing is, I am an equal opportunity conflict avoider. I would often pull this stunt with God too, and to be honest, on occasion, I still do. He never falls for it. He'll come looking for me every single time I run silent. Bless Him! I'm learning a better way, but recognizing this about myself is a huge help at this stage of my life. I'm finally getting it. Surrender isn't optional; it's unavoidable.

To be fair, I understand you're most likely not like me; people have different ways of viewing and experiencing surrender which makes it easier or harder to swallow. Whether you're as familiar with surrender as I am or not, it's still something you'll have to work out because it's a huge part of life after the fire. I can testify; crazy things will happen. Unexplainable pain will catch up to you at some point, no matter how well you think you can serpentine around it. Please take time to figure this out. You'll be needing it, and the fact that you're reading this book may be a tip off that you'll be needing it sooner than you think.

I had it all planned out. At forty, I left everything and everyone familiar to give ten years of my life teaching English overseas as a different way to live out my faith. After five years, the Holy Spirit prevented me from signing up for another year. Whoa! I hadn't seen that coming! I was finally making real friends, learning enough of the language to clearly communicate, and enjoying a season of spiritual growth and open doors for ministry around me. It just didn't add up. I said my tearful goodbyes, and in a fog of trust-without-understanding, I promised to return.

The following summer, with great joy, I did return for a visit. However, upon my arrival, I became frustrated beyond words...words I couldn't have spoken if I wanted to because I had lost my voice. I was there to conduct a two-day event and yet, I had no voice. Nothing. A friend traveling with me filled in the first day and all went well. But when the second day rolled around, I felt the Holy Spirit gently suggest we needed to change our schedule and location. It's a good thing we did, because within the hour, our meeting was interrupted by local officials. We were able to answer difficult questions honestly because we had subjected our best laid plans to not much more than a nudge.

By the time we were released to leave, two things occurred to me. First, if I had stayed and not returned home the previous year, much more would have been at stake from my disobedience. Additionally, if I had been unwilling to submit our plans to those of the Holy Spirit, the ripple effect of our encounter would have been far reaching. That day, I didn't preach a sermon that saved a city, but I was obedient. Surrendered.

Surrender won't be a thing of the past once you're off the wheel and out of the fire. Your bursts of surrender, your struggles to surrender, and your habit-forming commitment to surrender are not in vain. Surrender leads to fulfilling your life's mission, which is simply to be yourself in a way that brings glory to Jesus.

This is your mission, should you choose to accept it.

THE MISSION

"How do I live my life in a way that brings glory to Jesus?" Well, I'm so glad you asked.

Don't overthink this; I've tried not to oversimply it, but I keep coming back to this bottom line. Spend enough time with Jesus that He can see Himself in you. Whatever amount that is, that's it. Seeing Himself in you brings Him glory. To realize this, some of us will require more time in His presence than others; let's blame that on our personality and prior habits. Whatever it takes. That's the mission.

This happens through prayer and other spiritual disciplines as they come to you. Build a strong relationship with Jesus—a bond that nothing can separate. No thing and no one. Not death or life, angels or demons, fears for today or worries for tomorrow, powers of hell or the unseen world, or anything in all of creation can separate you from this bond of love and care with God made possible because of Jesus.[2] In other words, while you do have to put forth some effort, Jesus does a lot of the heavy lifting.

As your relationship grows, you'll find yourself knowing more of who you are in Him. This will enable you to serve, saying yes when you can and no when you can't, which I'm guessing would be a huge relief for so many who struggle with saying no. This bond of love between the human and Divine is real, palpable, even for someone like me, which is great news for someone like you.

Keep the mission at the center. Live to make His name great! Be who He intends you to be, not comparing yourself to anyone else,[3] and that'll do. That'll do just fine.

ONCE UPON A CERAMICS SHOP

When I was younger, my aunt owned a ceramics shop. She didn't throw clay on a wheel, but rather, she poured liquid slip, a kind of grey clay into molds. She had hundreds of them. Molds were everywhere. She would miraculously find the ones she wanted like needles in haystacks, fill them, turn them out, and let the resulting greenware dry a little before cleaning them. She would glaze and fire them, or fire-to-bisque certain pieces, paint them out, and then sell them or give them as gifts.

She let me help at the shop when I would visit during the summer. I wasn't always the most helpful niece. I was a bit clumsy and broke my fair share of pieces. In my defense, sometimes the unfired greenware was extremely fragile and the slightest bump would knock off an edge. But when I did things just right, the pieces turned out like I imagined they would. To me, the process was fascinating. Knowing the dynamics was empowering and made me want to create even more. If I read them right, the looks of appreciation on the faces of those who received my little trinkets as gifts was a huge satisfaction.

Believe me when I tell you, nothing could have induced me to destroy my little masterpieces. The care I took in packing them for transport a mile down the road to my grandma's house bordered on the ridiculous. And if I, an amateur, felt that strongly about my creations, you must know the Master Potter, Creator of the universe, is not interested in destroying you. Not in the least.

But alas, sometimes we crack, we chip, and we break, don't we? Yes, sometimes it feels as if my life has been whacked by a huge cosmic hammer, or vigorously shaken like a powdered health drink. In either extreme and for every notch in-between, blaming the Potter seems natural, but railing against Him makes no logical sense nor spiritual sense either.

So what can we do about our brokenness? I'll give you a hint. Accept it, and don't hide it.

BROKEN

Brokenness: it's not such a bad thing, according to one particularly famous giant killer, also known as the man after God's own heart, also known as an adulterer and murderer, also known as a shepherd king. David wrote that the LORD is close to the brokenhearted and that He rescues those whose spirits are crushed.[4] That's not to say that I'd camp out in line for a dose of it like those die-hard Apple fans did for the first several iPhones. But in my experience, I would have to agree, it seems in the times I've been the most brokenhearted, the LORD of my life has been close; and when I thought my spirit was crushed beyond recovery, He rescued me.

One such time was when I dropped out of university at the age of eighteen. I failed two out of four courses my first semester because I didn't know how to drop a class and was petrified to ask. Ironically, one of the courses was Computer Science. It's ironic because most of the people who know me could attest to the fact that I know my way around a computer. It felt like my immaturity was on full display for all the world to see. It was painful and incredibly embarrassing. As the first in my family to head off to college, I wasn't exactly setting the bar very high for those coming behind me. What an epic fail. A friend at the time encouraged me by saying, "sometimes you gotta quit to win." Yep, I'd say that's pretty crushed.

In hindsight, it did allow me to walk through another door. I spent a few years doing short-term missions work in the Philippines with my family before returning to the States to give higher education another go. I learned a valuable lesson through all that: it's okay for me to ask questions when I don't know what to do. Even though I was nervous to go back to school, afraid to fail again, it turned out to be the right path for me.

Years later, I met a Chinese evangelist. She asked for prayer and then explained to our little group, complete strangers to her, that she had been struggling with a spiritually-stony heart for years and was praying for a heart of flesh as promised to God's people in the book of Ezekiel.[5] In that moment, I was struck with the vulnerability of her confession and admired it greatly. I could tell she was someone who could minister from a position of authenticity. Though she was an evangelist who had suffered persecution and experienced things I cannot imagine, she didn't pretend to know it all or come off as spiritually superior. It made me want to hear more, be more

10

like that. Perhaps on that day, more than any other day I can recall, vulnerability hit my radar. I didn't know what to do about it at the time, but I tucked it away, praying for further information.

In recent years, the work of research professor Brené Brown has given us much to consider about our view of vulnerability. Her 2011 TED talk on the subject, "The Power of Vulnerability," is one of the top five TED talks in history. Clearly, I was not the only one interested. So many of us perceive the very notion of vulnerability as being weak, but I'm learning that this idea is a cultural bias. As it turns out, vulnerability is the antidote to perfectionism and hypocrisy. It's a braver way to live than trying to hold things together in pride without the help of others and dare I say, God Himself.

Being broken gives me a chance to be authentic, making real connections with others. It can release me to be vulnerable. It helps me let go of the curated persona I love to hide behind and bumps me out of the seat of judgement. Quite frankly, it helps keep me from getting too big for my britches. And when I see vulnerability in others, it is cause for admiration. When I see it in myself, though it makes me want to avert my eyes, it's proof that I'm showing up as I am, a sinner saved by grace. It doesn't mean I'm weak. It means I'm human and redeemable by a God who values the ones He makes.

After all, I am not a Starbucks cup that's discarded after one use. I'm not even a plastic fork that got washed by accident instead of being thrown away.

I am made for real life. Eternal life, where my weaknesses will one day be a thing of the past.

As the greatly-esteemed apostle Paul wrote, it's in our weaknesses that God shows His strength.[6] I'm certain God gets to showcase His strength on a regular basis with me because my weaknesses are many and they keep me from taking any of His credit.

Brokenness might challenge my sense of wholeness, but it's really not the end of my world. It is a season that shows God is at work in my life. He chooses to use broken things. Cue Dante Bowe's song, "Potter and Friend"; skip to the bridge where he repeats, "You take broken things and make them beautiful. You take broken things and put them back together again."[7] That's my refrain.

He chose to use a broken me. It's His way.

When the outside of a seed is broken, the inside can push its way out. When chains are broken, those in bondage go free. When addictions and strongholds are broken, there is deliverance. When negative thought patterns are broken, behavior changes and DNA is recoded. Brokenness isn't all bad, but your opinion of it usually depends on where you are in your understanding of the process.

BROKEN THINGS IN SCRIPTURE

As I prepared for writing this section, a few things in Scripture came to mind that were broken before they were of enough significance to be mentioned in there. After further research, my list grew. It's good to know there's hope for the broken!

- **Jacob's hip**: It was wrenched out of its socket before he was renamed Israel. (Genesis 32:25-28)
- **Job's health**: In addition to the heartbreak of losing his children, Job endured broken health as a testimony of His faith in God, even when he didn't understand what was going on. (Job 9:17)
- **A Rock**: Moses struck a rock and as it broke open, water sprung out to quench the thirst of the Israelites in the desert. (Exodus 17:6)
- **Gideon's Pitchers**: Gideon's army broke pitchers to reveal lights encircling their enemy's camp so God could receive the credit for a victory. (Judges 7:20)
- **A Proud King**: Babylonian king Nebuchadnezzar was brought down and broken by God to bring about worship and admiration of God's name. (Daniel 4:27, 33-34)
- **Five Loaves**: Five thousand were fed when Jesus blessed and broke five loaves of bread. (Matthew 14:19)
- **Alabaster box**: Mary broke it, releasing a perfumed oil which was poured over the head of Jesus, preparing Him for burial. (Matthew 26:7, 12)
- **Body of Jesus**: He was broken for those who follow Him. (1 Corinthians 11:23-24)

There you have it: proof God uses the broken. And all the while, He is there with me—in me.

As someone who lives at least a few millennia removed from these verses but wants to be in sync with them, I have wondered at how being broken serves any purpose in my life. If I am created as His masterpiece,[8] how does allowing me to be marred bring God the glory He created me to bring? Could it be that in order for rivers of living water to flow, there must be a breaking of the vessel it's in?[9] In order for love and compassion to flow from my stony heart, perhaps I am the kind of person who needs to be broken open, giving way to a softer interior life. I have to believe there is purpose for His process.

I wonder if Paul had this idea in mind when he wrote his first letter to the Corinthians. He said, and I paraphrase, God uses things the world considers foolish in order to shame those who think they are wise. And He chooses things that are powerless to shame those who are powerful.[10] If I continue in his logic, the following statement makes perfect sense: God uses the broken to shame those who are trying to keep it all together on their own. Not at all words I want to hear if I'm afraid of breaking, music to my ears if I'm in pieces.

WHEN THE POTTER ALLOWS THE BREAKING

We ask God a lot of questions, don't we? Probably one of the biggest and most often used is "why?" Why didn't I get the raise at work? Why did You let me go through that valley? Why did that officer pull me over for speeding when I was on my way to church? Why did I have to go through that as a kid? It's okay to ask why, but I discovered something as I tried my hand at *kintsugi*. It was that discovery that changed the way I see God and how He allows things to happen in my life.

I was mildly intrigued by the method of *kintsugi* and I wanted to experience the process for myself. At first, I Googled and YouTubed my bleary-eyed self into the wee hours of the morning on several occasions. I searched Etsy and eventually Amazon.com for *kintsugi* kits. When my kit arrived from Spain, yes Spain, it contained a few sticks, a double-barreled syringe of two-part epoxy, a pair of large, rubber gloves, and a pouch of gold powder. I was all set except for one thing. I didn't have anything to repair.

Rather than ransacking my cabinets to reenact the Greek custom of slamming dishes to the ground for kicks at special events, I went shopping, purchased a few inexpensive rice bowls and brought them home. I fished out a hammer from my toolbox and tried to tease out how I was going to break that bowl without it going into a million pieces. I wrapped it in paper, then cushioned it with a doubled-up blanket. I was trying to avoid making a mosaic. After all, I wanted a bowl, not a sculpture as my end result.

The first whack bounced off the blanket with no effect. The second whack did the same. So, I held my breath and gave that bowl a solid smack with the hammer and I felt it give way. I quickly unwrapped the bowl, and with relief, exhaled as I saw it was in a few, clean broken pieces.

To be honest, breaking the bowl was the hardest part of the entire process for me. I sense perhaps that encapsulates the way God views our breaking processes too.

If I'm not careful, I can let my imagination run away with itself, conjuring up this huge hammer of God whaling against an unprotected little me, threatening to smash me to bits. I might even think I deserve it. But if the breaking of me is anything like the breaking of that bowl, God takes every precaution to retain the integrity of who He made me to be. He truly isn't trying to destroy me, but to break me in a way that will bring Him glory. My ability to surrender and trust Him keeps me in the process.

CARELESS HANDLERS

Recently, while visiting my mom, I offered to unset and then reset the table before supper. She's someone who likes to have her table set with seasonal decorations when the table isn't in use. As I was removing a ceramic place setting, I got distracted. I knew the little cup wasn't balanced steadily in its place on the plate, but before I could react, that little guy slid right off the plate and went sailing to crash-land on the kitchen floor. I wouldn't call the final result a clean break. It was in pieces. I broke out in a sweat.

As you can imagine, I felt horrible! Even worse, it was a piece from my aunt's ceramic shop, a piece of high sentimental value. I scrambled to collect as many pieces as I could as quickly as possible, because in the background, I could hear my mom saying, "Just throw it away," as the broom inched nearer my position. I couldn't bear the thought of not trying to *kintsugi* it back to life. This was the result.

It brought her smiles when she opened it as a gift the other day. She said she suspected I would try.

She didn't mind the gold trails running here and there around the cup. She was happy to have it back in one piece again and was glad I didn't give up and throw it away.

Though I'd been careless with that cup, it was of more value after having been repaired, because it came so close to having been lost. When someone asks what happened to it, the highlight won't be of how it was broken, but of how it was repaired. I'm no *kintsugi* master, but that cup now points back to me. Its story and my story are now intertwined.

What about when I'm careless with myself? This is when I don't make time for important things, when I get too busy preferring everyone ahead of myself to the detriment of myself, when I say things I don't really mean in a moment of insecurity, and when my health suffers because of poor decisions. Hairline cracks appear on the surface when I am careless to believe what the enemy says about me rather than what the Word says. Negative self-talk and neglecting time alone with God puts stress on my soul.

I don't know what your careless tendencies are, but you've got them. We all do. When you find yourself broken from them, get into the Master Potter's hands and let Him put you back together again.

In His hands, there's no room for beating yourself up.

Jesus puts us back together again as we acknowledge and confess our brokenness, renew our mind, and in other words, change it—also called repentance—and take steps to change a negative pattern through the power of the Holy Spirit.

What about when I'm careless with others? When my lack of attention, withdrawal in a relationship, or sitting in judgment causes harm to my fellow jars of clay, how should I respond? Should I ignore my part in it to avoid conflict? Pretend it wasn't my fault? Provide inventive excuses for my actions? I should probably learn from my mistakes. Make amends. Be part of the repair process if possible. I am challenged by this thought to pay careful attention to the way I handle others in my life so that I don't cause harm. And when I do, take responsibility for my actions and make things right.

And finally, let's flip the coin. When I am the one who is handled carelessly by others, what is my response? Is it, "Just throw me away now! I'm ruined. Nobody will want me anyway." Perhaps you're more the polar opposite, "Nobody treats me this way and gets away with it," or something in-between? I know what my knee-jerk reaction is. What's yours?

I want my response to smack of generosity and forgiveness. Generosity that gives the benefit of the doubt and forgiveness that sets me free from bitterness.

Accidental breaks do happen. Forgiveness is required and surrender of unhealthy patterns is key.

MALICIOUS BREAKS

I've never understood the fascination some people have with poking at insects, intentionally maiming them to see what happens. I just don't get intentionally hurting animals, people, or bugs; I can't fathom it. It would bring me no joy or satisfaction. While I can't speak to having malicious intent, I do have to contend with those who maliciously intend harm toward me.

When I was in third grade, I had somewhat-of-a-friend from England. I think I put up with her because I loved hearing her accent, but that's about it. One day she, another girl, and I were walking home from school when she turned suddenly and shoved me as hard as she could into prickly bushes beneath the trees by our apartment. She left me there and continued her walk home without me. I sat there a minute, stunned, hardly believing what I had just experienced. It was as malicious as it was effective. I didn't ever find out why she shoved me, and I avoided her like the plague afterwards. That same year my family moved, and I changed schools. Because of her, I was wary of making new friends. As a child, I felt every inch of that betrayal.

Malicious things can be much more sinister than this, much, much more. Sadly, most of the coping mechanisms we employ as children are outdated for use as adults, but we keep doing what we know to do until we learn to do something else. So, what do we do when we are cracked, chipped, or broken by the intentional mistreatment of others?

Are you doing the same things you did as a kid? Is it working for you?

Thankfully, as I matured, I outgrew the story of the English girl. I didn't feel betrayed by total strangers for long. I was able to reset my mind back to the original way I approached people with openness and a general belief that people are good. If I hadn't moved on from that third-grade mentality and coping strategy of complete avoidance, my life would look very different today. The precious friendships I have now might never have formed.

As for the more serious malicious attacks, yes, I've had them. I've spent much time on the Master Potter's repair bench. Trust me when I tell you, there is a lot of forgiveness involved in getting over a malicious attack; don't expect it to be easy. Forgiveness of myself, forgiveness of the person with malicious intent, and even to an extent, "forgiveness of God"...lots and lots of forgiveness. I may not always be able to forget, but I can drop it, let it go, and stop obsessing. This is a choice; and for some of us, it is a learned behavior. It is surrender in action. For me, I know forgiveness is taking root and bitterness is on its way out when I don't feel its heat rise within me, and when I can stop obsessing and analyzing every angle of the malicious break.

Sticks and stones may break my bones, but it's words that can nearly kill me. Malicious words thud against my breastplate, rattling my cage. False accusations hurled at my reputation nearly knock my knees out from under me. But as a person in relationship with Jesus, I address these realities, knowing that what He says about me is the final word. I am His. I am His delight. I realize His words are true. In my weakness, He is my strength.

Along with everyone else, He sees my flaws and weaknesses. He sees the chips, cracks, and breaks, but He knows how to mend them.

BROKEN OR SHATTERED

I made an interesting observation as I tried my hand at *kintsugi*. I noticed that different kinds of ceramics and pottery have different breaking points. Bowls that looked nearly identical on the outside would break differently under the same intensity of "whack" from the hammer.

In reflecting on this, I've drawn a few conclusions.

First, if God is allowing me to be broken, it doesn't do me any good to resist. As the pressure mounts, I could shatter. While He can certainly repair me after I'm shattered, it may have been avoided if I'd surrendered to Him at first. Why cause more trouble for myself? Note to future self: stop resisting.

Second, I resolve to surrender and be easily broken by God, as well as resistant to breaking caused by the careless or malicious acts of others. I will not disengage to avoid the pain of being broken, but I will rely on the Holy Spirit to direct me. I will yield to God and His body on earth, but I will resist the devil so that no weapon formed against me will prosper.[11]

I don't want to find myself somewhere in the midst of the sermon, "Sinners in the Hands of an Angry God," by Jonathan Edwards. Though it sparked a spiritual awakening in the mid-1700s, the only thing it sparks in me is a willingness to cry "UNCLE!" to my heavenly Potter before the ten-count gets to two.

SURRENDER

If I get to choose between being broken or shattered, broken is looking like a pretty good option to me.

THE REPAIR PROCESS

You already know this if you read the little parable at the beginning of this book, but the original *kintsugi* repair process was just that: a process. A long one. It's a great metaphor to remind me that when I'm broken, I can't just act as if nothing happened, or fake it till I make it. I must acknowledge the process and stay in it if I want to reap the promises of God for my life.

As we go through the stages of grief, the steps of recovery, the work of rebuilding a relationship, or other reconstructing of our spirit, we must keep in mind that these things don't happen overnight. I know microwave popcorn is awesome, especially with extra butter. And the movies that download to your phone in minutes are amazing, but those metaphors won't work for how the repair process takes place.

We aren't zapped back together. We surrender to our Heavenly Potter, not to that other Potter guy with the wand.

I used to love stealing away to ride my brother's skateboard in the neighborhood. At the time, we lived in a hilly area and those hills were very tempting to ride like a downward twisting wave. The huffing and puffing required to get to the top of those hills was worth it in the rush back down. Imagine this though. House rules were that I couldn't ride the skateboard on the road—so I had to use the sidewalk—and I couldn't ride the big hill in front of our house. Add the fact that the wheels were metal. Yes, you read that right. They were metal. We never got around to upgrading them. Every time I got on that board, I was literally one pebble away from serious road rash.

Praise the Lamb, the road rash didn't get me. But my clumsiness did.

One morning on holiday, standing at the edge of our lawn, I jammed my foot on the back end of the board to kick it up as I headed back into the house. I tripped and fell flat on my face. My arms shot forward to break the fall. And my left arm snapped. When I went to get up, I realized both bones broke and apparently one of them had broken through the skin, pulling dirt back into the hole it had made in my arm. Gross, right? Thankfully there was no blood. I freaked out just the same; that was one gnarly arm.

Just getting to the hospital was a process. After they set my arm, I stayed on in my own little room there for a week. Going to the bathroom was a new challenge, a process. Finding clothes that would fit around the cast was a process. Everything I did was a process. The cast came in handy for blocking during football, but outside of that, I wanted it off. NOW!

They had to cut a hole in the cast to keep checking the wound made by the bone...the one that came out. They cut the hole with an electric saw after telling me to be very, very still as it buzzed in the background. That was scary; I was warned not to even flinch. When the cast came off after many weeks, learning to use my left arm again was a process.

Living a *kintsugi* life is a process. I think you get it. There's no way around it. Life after the fire will lead to a breaking point if you want to be used by God; and living a *kintsugi* life means He puts you back together in His way and in His time.

And you don't always know every bit of It. Sometimes when you think you're done, there's another step you don't anticipate.

KEEPING HOPE ALIVE

As you go through your *kintsugi* life, you will discover that keeping hope alive through the process will, at times, be a challenge. What is hope? Brené Brown describes it as a way of *thinking* that will produce behaviors to help you navigate your circumstances.[12] Learning the truth of that last sentence was an "ah-hah!" moment for me. For years, I thought hope was a positive feeling or an emotional response to a situation. Therefore, when I didn't *feel* hopeful, I struggled to believe the possibility that tomorrow would be any different from today. Now that I have moved hope from the feeling category to the thinking category, I can consciously decide to exercise my hope. I'm no longer a victim of my emotions, or the lack of them.

This is exciting to me, because it means I can train my brain to hope. As my thinking changes, so will my behaviors and expectations. The voice of the pessimist in me is finally overtaken by the voice of my inner optimist as I stay in the process of becoming whole. The amazing part of all this cognitive activity is what happens when I kick it up a notch by verbalizing my hope aloud. That's when my faith is impacted.

In her book, *Switch on Your Brain*, Caroline Leaf, a cognitive neuroscientist and Christian, explains how "what you think with your *mind* changes your brain and body...your mind is a switch."[13] Finding that switch and flipping it on is a powerful discovery. For those of you who appreciate how science proves Scripture, this one's for you. When I profess with my mouth what I know is true, whether I *feel* it to be true or not, my brain is convinced by the sound of my own voice. The exercise of healthy self-talk actually gives hope the elbow room it needs to do its work.

As a result of a firm decision to keep hope alive, I'm able get a glimpse of where I'm headed by the grace of God. I am also willing to persist in the face of adversity, failure, and pain. Ultimately, I have a witness in my spirit that I will be whole because the One who started a good work in me will be faithful to complete it;[14] I just have to stick with the process even when I don't feel like it.

As you begin to notice the effects of the Master Potter as He mends your brokenness, the key element you'll need in order to keep hope alive is persistence, the tenacity to make it through. If you struggle with perfectionism, this can be a tough one, because life can get messy when your rough edges need sanding down. For those who think failure is the end, it will be an education in getting back up no matter how many times you fall down. Yes, you must have faith in God, but you'll also need faith in yourself to endure. In her book, *The Gifts of Imperfection*, Brené Brown argues that we can't let the culture of "fun, fast and easy" derail us. Hang in there! In the words of James, the half-brother of Jesus Himself, "when your endurance is fully developed, you will be perfect and complete."[15]

Now, as I end this section, let me take you briefly on a little rabbit trail.

When I'm in struggle, in addition to zeroing in on Scripture that fuels me, I find it helps to listen intentionally to songs of encouragement. When I'm stumbling on the pathway to a goal, or when I realize I need to recalibrate my plans, I am tempted to stall out. As I work to keep hope alive, in the midst of enduring, it helps to keep my mind on positive things. The apostle Paul himself recommended as much.[16] There are many songs out there that encourage me, but the Sangary Brothers' song "Trust the Process," puts everything into perspective. I am infused with hope from above when "coincidentally" the music I'm listening to fits the season I'm in. Ever had someone suggest a song to you that was just what you needed?

#bonusgraceforthejourney

On a practical note, when I need to generate a little positive self-talk, these are a few of my favorite go-to phrases of hope. I don't just think them. I speak them aloud or under my breath in a whisper. These words are virtually impotent until they are uttered, heard with my ears and lodged in my brain. I say things like:

"Tomorrow is another day. It will be better."

"Sweetie, you'll be okay." (Yes, I say this to myself.)

"I *will* get back up."

"Messy is okay."

"It's not the end of the world, Ang [insert your name here]."

"Lord, You are my strength. Thanks for being You!"

"More mercy, please."

Different seasons of life require different truths. What positive phrases help you get through your seasons of struggle?

As a central theme for Christians to latch onto, be encouraged to sink your hook into hope; it is a strong and trustworthy anchor[17] that leads us into God's presence which happens to be where there is fullness of joy.[18]

WE CAN'T FIX OURSELVES

Remember the rice bowls I mentioned purchasing earlier? Well, it's the strangest thing; not one of them repaired themselves. Everything that was needed was sitting right there on the table with them, but it doesn't appear they even tried.

Obviously.

A decade ago, if I had been a bowl on that table, I would have reached for the resin! Why wait for someone else when I might be able to fix myself? I didn't want to be a bother to anyone. Not even to God. True story.

We all have our way of trying to fix ourselves, hide ourselves, and improve ourselves to some degree. What we can do on our own might be good enough to get us through this life, but it won't pass the test to get us into the next. The complete repair and healing we're looking for is found by surrendering to the process under the watchful eye and competent hands of the Master Potter. This Jesus is not like anyone else you've ever encountered! You can't frustrate Him or overload Him. It's not possible.

He sees me as a masterpiece when I can't. He sees the void that needs to be filled, lurking just beyond my line of sight. He can reach those places in me that I can't reach myself. I'm too much for myself to handle on my own. He's the One I need. Nobody else can handle me either to the extent I crave. Just Him.

For all of us who are part of His body here on Earth, it's not our job to fix those around us, but we can be His hands. It's fascinating how Jesus enables me to reach out when I don't even know what to do or say. How He helps me engage when my amygdala is screaming, "Danger! Flight!" I can't fix you; you can't fix me, but when we are His hands, it's a thing of Divine beauty. It brings immense glory to God as He sees Himself in us.

GIVING GOD ALL THE PIECES

When I committed to put this book together, I got so excited about the material. During one particular conversation, a friend shared an interesting story with me that I just have to pass along. Someone who was tired of trying to fix herself in a season of brokenness finally cried out to God saying, "Please help me! I can't do this anymore." And He responded! He responded by saying, "Can do! I've been waiting. But you've got to give me *all* the pieces."

All the pieces!

Sometimes I find it a challenge to find all the pieces when I break something. Sometimes I've got to move furniture, or squat down and peer under a table with a flashlight angled just right. And sometimes I step on them in the dark and hop around for a while saying nonsense under my breath.

I think what He was getting at was that she needed to be willing to pour out all her hurt in His presence. And sometimes, that's work; it takes time. Giving Him all the pieces often means going to a dark place inside that you'd rather not go. It's remembering things you'd rather forget. It's fessing up.

Those pieces you are hiding from Him are being hidden for a reason; figuring out what that reason is and facing it is what allows you to release your death grip on them and hand them over.

Got any that popped into your mind?

Have a nagging sense that this is where you're at?

Then take some time to explore what step to take next as you surrender to Him *all* the pieces of your brokenness.

Aaaaaaand we're back to surrender.

Now that we're here, I can hardly wait for you to let me share with you the joys that come from being *kintsugi'd* by the Master Potter of the universe.

PART 2: FILLED

KINTSUGI REPAIR

I was pleasantly surprised to discover there are three basic methods of repair used in *kintsugi*, and the terminology for each type of repair blew my mind in light of this project. In fact, it was the terminology that proved to be the tipping point of my putting this book together.

In most *kintsugi*, only one or two types of repair are employed, but in special situations, and for an even more aesthetically pleasing result, a third method is used. Even now, I can hardly contain my excitement to share these details with you, so let's dive in.

REPAIR TYPE 1: HIBI - FILLED

Hibi is the most common type of repair. Resin is mixed with a little flour and used to fuse pieces back together and to fill the cracks. It's the basic starting point for all other types of repair.

When we are filled with the Holy Spirit, the process of becoming whole begins. The very Spirit of Jesus begins filling the cracks in our lives as we allow Him to work in us. From the moment you are filled with the Holy Spirit, as God looks at you and sees Himself running throughout your spirit like the golden trails of a *kintsugi* repair, it is a pure delight to Him. He sees you as you are and also as you will be.[19] What an incredible truth. We are beautiful in His eyes, even with our imperfections; it is those imperfections that make Him shine.

Being filled with the Holy Spirit is just the starting point of a new life in Christ Jesus. It's the beginning, a foundational condition for all other work of the Holy Spirit in our lives. If you are seeking wholeness, allowing the very Spirit of Jesus to fill you daily is a necessary spiritual practice. This is made possible with prayer that centers on acknowledging one's need for God and taking time to listen for His voice.

Yes, there are seasons of my life when it is a challenge for me to stay mindful of my need to be filled each day. However, when my spiritual awareness is sharpened by the Holy Spirit, I experience benefits that impact my daily life. I find I am more sensitive to the needs of others, I'm more willing to obey or observe what God is speaking to me, and I'm more appreciative, worshipful, and grateful for how God is working in my life.

As I look back on my spiritual journey, I can see a steady progression.

As a child, I loved Jesus. I tried, and often failed, to do all the things people said He would like kids to do. I wasn't very good at it, but I hung in there. It wasn't until I was in my teens that I realized Jesus had been the One hanging in there with me. I started to wake up to my personal need for spiritual discernment and guidance.

As I hit my twenties, the reason behind such things as prayer and Bible reading started to make more sense to me as I got plugged into Jesus as my source of strength; "adulting" can do that to a person. I committed more of my life, talent, and time to Jesus in my thirties, and that's when He began to show up in the places I needed Him most.

In my forties, I continued to let Jesus run in all directions of my life, filling every space He could, and His ministry through me expanded. Now that I'm into my fifties, I'm so excited that He's still at work in my life, teaching me and showing me how much He cares deeply for me. He is continually strengthening me, fortifying the places I once shored up on my own.

As I mature physically and spiritually, I've noticed my focus is less on what I can do for God, and more on how I can get closer to Him effectively. In a manner of speaking, I've raised my gaze from His hands to His face. At this stage of my life, I'm discovering that staying filled means I have to back off of some of the things I was able to do when I was younger simply because my energy level has changed, and my priorities have shifted. If I don't slow down at least a little, I am the kind of person who tends to let other responsibilities squeeze out my personal time with God. I choose not to go into autopilot mode as I turn the last few corners of my race here on earth. I recognize my need to live full of the Holy Spirit in every stage, even if it looks a little different from the outside.

Living a life filled by the Holy Spirit enables us to fulfill our purpose, which is ultimately a close relationship with God. Not only does this bring Him immense glory, but it becomes the foundation of our spiritual transformation into true sons and daughters of God.[20]

Several years ago, I asked a simple question: "What did people in the Bible do who were 'filled with the Spirit?'" The results are pretty interesting. I put it this way in the *7 Essentials of Kids Prayer 2.0*, "Prophesying, singing, dancing, edifying, speaking in tongues, boldness, and even walking into a wilderness are expressions of fullness and are recorded in Scripture. Incidentally, each expression is connected in some way to bringing glory to God."[21] The Holy Spirit doesn't turn us into spiritual clones. He awakens in us the vision and ability to fulfill our own destiny the way Jesus fulfilled His. His Spirit joins with our spirit, making us joint heirs with Christ.[22]

I am not meant to *be* Jesus. I am meant to *be* Angie. And not just any old Angie, but the Angie who is secure, whose weaknesses He makes strong because He fills me to the brim.

REPAIR TYPE 2: KAKE NO KINTSUGI RE - MISSING PIECE

Previously, I mentioned how it's important to give God all the pieces of our brokenness, not holding anything back from Him. So, what if there's still a missing piece we can't seem to put our finger on?

In *kintsugi*, the void left by a small missing piece is filled in with resin, covered in lacquer, and finished off with gold. When we have a missing piece, Jesus can totally fill the void. Whether that void is left by a hard season of life, a colossal disappointment, a dysfunctional relationship, a death, or any other thing, Jesus is enough. Our willingness to let Him be enough is an important part of surrendering to His process. At the end of the day, we are breathing to bring Him glory; and sometimes, I know, even breathing is hard when the wind is knocked out of us.

Are you looking for a missing piece? Childhood trauma and the resulting coping patterns we develop to protect ourselves are guideposts indicating a starting place to look. If you have a painful event that led to a painful emotion which caused you to say, "never again," start looking there. More than likely, that painful event caused you to believe something about yourself that is in conflict with who God says you are. As soon as you are able, I encourage you to choose to believe you are who He says you are and not what your past has named you; then, look around. That void caused by a missing piece will begin filling up with His golden truth. And if you find a shattered remnant hiding in the chaos of a painful past, be sure you hand it over to the One who knows how, when, and where to use it best.

Living out that last paragraph is a lot of work! But from personal experience, I can tell you, it works. In my mid-twenties, I experienced a lot of upheaval in my life concerning my career path and it left a few marks. It took me some time, as in years, to locate a couple of those elusive missing pieces, but when I handed them over, transformation began.

I still needed proof that this spiritual process of giving God all the pieces actually works. Talking theory doesn't cut it for me. After nearly twenty years of handing those pieces over, I finally got a glimmer of what was happening on the inside of me.

While visiting a friend, her dad called me over and took my hand. He waited until I looked him in the eye, then as I recall, he said, "Angie, I've been watching you for a while now, and I've noticed a hole in your heart. But it looks different now. It's filling up. It's fillin' right up. Keep on doing what you're doing. You're gonna be alright." There it was: literal proof that transformation was taking place.

You may not have the same experience, but God will figure out a way to let you know how you're progressing. He really does care for you and knows how to speak the language of your heart.

What about the missing piece representing how we spend our adult years? Will I be married? Will I remain single? Yep, it's a biggie! As you can imagine, it can be a monumental struggle to surrender this area to Jesus so He can perform a "Missing Piece" repair, whether it's temporary or permanent.

Many of us grow up with expectations of marrying a soul mate that hasn't yet materialized. It can be confusing and at least a little frustrating! So, let's look at the facts logically. In 1960, 72% of people over the age of 18 were married. That number has decreased to only 50% in 2016 and is holding steady with a growing number of adults who never marry. Not only are less people getting married, but the average age for marriage has increased from 21 in 1960 to 28 in 2016.[23] Does this help you put anything into perspective?

If you're reading this and feel even a slight tinge of guilt for making a single adult feel "less than" because he or she isn't married yet, there's no immediate need to run to the nearest altar to repent with a dramatic flair. But at the very least, you may want to adjust your thinking and soften your approach. If you're reading this as a single adult who is just dying to get married, are you tired of waiting or stuck concerning your plans for the future? Then I trust these statistics help relieve a little pressure. I hope they provide you with a clearer vantage point from which to see where you're headed. You're not totally out of options or time!

I know from personal experience that it can be difficult to make plans for the future without knowing how this particular missing piece will be found...or filled.

Have you heard the story, or the Greek myth actually, of how humans once walked the earth whole, and then were split into male and female halves as a punishment? According to the myth, both male and female have been seeking to find their other half ever since. It may feel this way at times, but I'm glad this is simply a myth; in other words, I'm glad it's not true. It's not based on truth. No human can complete another human. We humans are made complete in Christ.

As a single adult myself, I'd like to mention just a few things about the "missing piece" syndrome singles face.

First, marriage does not equal maturity. Just because someone gets married, it doesn't mean they're automatically mature enough to do so. And conversely, if someone doesn't marry, it doesn't mean they're somehow forever immature. I cheer for all the marriages that make it; I aspire to be the kind of spouse someone could love forever, the kind who loves in spite of. But my marital status is not an indicator of my emotional or spiritual maturity; unless it's in light of how obedient I am concerning how I follow Jesus.

Rather than pine for some elusive idea of marital bliss, I can choose to let Jesus fill that void until it's time for someone else to stand in that gap. Yes, Lord! And if that time never comes, I can choose to live filled by, and satisfied in, Jesus.[24] I can truly be satisfied in Him.

I'm not less if I'm single; I'm not more if I'm married. Boom! That's me dropping the mic.

Second, singleness doesn't equal loneliness. I've heard married people talk about feeling lonely in their marriage, so I can logically deduce marriage isn't the answer to feeling lonely. So what is? From my experience, I have come to believe loneliness is a symptom of misguided thinking which leads to isolation. To combat this, we identify the lie that's isolating us and replace it with the truth found in God's Word. For me, misguided thinking can stem from something as simple as failing to acknowledge Jesus is the only One who can satisfy the deep needs of my heart.

We are made for relationship and community. By honoring this need for community, to the extent of our healthy personality, we can live a life that's not withdrawn or riddled with lack. For some of us, a stable network of friends and extended family will define community while for others it will be having a spouse and children. Either way works for me; how about you?

I may not always be able to put my finger on a missing piece, but when I can, I surrender it to God—giving Him *all* the pieces. When I can't, I invite and trust Him to fill the void that causes me distress. As He fills each void in my life, the pain gives way to the comfort of His love. It's such a joy to acknowledge Him and testify to others of what He can do.

BITTERNESS

Bitterness is a slippery business. At the very least, it dulls the shine that Jesus brings when He fills a gaping hole. At worst, it behaves like an acid that eats right through the work of the Holy Spirit, keeping the gaping hole of a missing piece exposed.

This multisided nemesis is often introduced as a seed in my spirit when I perceive I've been treated unfairly. I deal with it on occasion in my relationships, in part because of how I interact with the world as someone who values fairness and peacemaking. I am in danger of bitterness "lodging in my craw," as some Southerners say, when I feel anger and disappointment, whether I express it or not. If I'm being honest, I experience these emotions most when I feel God is treating me unfairly. As resentment on steroids, bitterness is a corrosive toxin that I have to glove up and clean out. Numbing, binging, and denying are never a solution; but sometimes I do forget.

When I've done "this, this, and this" for God but He doesn't do that thing I've expected in return, I must watch for the dulling down of my fervor and listen for any crackling of the bitter acid eating away at my relationship with Jesus. I know academically that God's priority for me is not what's fair by my Western standards. If it was, He wouldn't have come to take on my sin and punishment because quite frankly, that's not fair, is it? Is it fair for someone else to pay for my weaknesses, my sin? Well, when I put it that way, nothing about all the things He's done in my life is fair. I can never return anything to the God of the universe for showing an interest in me. Or can I?

If God isn't as interested in my definition of fairness as I am, what is He interested in? He is interested in doing what's right by His standard.[25] Pretty much, when I peel away all the layers and "theo-speak," (you know, when someone uses theology as a fancy way to say simple things) it comes back to His interest in receiving glory from my life no matter the cost. I'm not helpless against God's will for my life. I get to choose my response.

I must remember that everything is not about me. He puts me in places and situations so that He will be noticed, perhaps to spark an inquiry that allows me to point others to Him. In return for His lavish "unfair" treatment of me, I give Him full access to work in my life. I trust Him, and I choose to see what some would call the "unfairness" of our relationship as a beautiful inequality, a glass nearly full rather than nearly empty. In order to do this, I have to change my thinking, which is something ultimately only I can do.

The first step to removing bitterness is to acknowledge it's there, calling it by name. Then assess what needs to happen next. Do I need to face a fear? Do I need to forgive someone, be it a perpetrator, God, or myself? Do I need to get out of the past and into the present? Once I've named bitterness, I can look at it from various perspectives to help me eradicate it. All of it.

One last thing. If you suspect bitterness in your own story or detect it in the story of someone else, understand that showering bitterness with sympathy is like pouring gasoline on a fire. Bitterness loves sympathy and will try to elbow its way into every conversation to drink it in.

While bitterness—that seed of perceived injustice that excuses my actions, attitudes, anger, harsh words, slander and other evil behavior—wants to be heard, it also wants to be left alone to grow. Paul admonished the Ephesians, and us, to get rid of it (Ephesians 4:31).

If sympathy isn't the answer, what is?

Empathy.

Unlike sympathy, which speaks from a safe distance and sounds an awful lot like judgment, empathy gets up close and personal. Rather than isolate, empathy connects. So, how can we tell the difference?

Empathy might sound like, "I see where you're coming from." It might even say, "I don't quite know what to say right now but thank you for sharing." It's kind and honest, but it won't "bless your heart." (Which is probably one of the least empathic responses...ever.)

Best of all, empathy allows me to connect without having to fix what's wrong with the other person. (Yes!) Leaning into someone else's discomfort can feel counterintuitive. It is a challenge for someone like me who seeks to bring peace and resolution to problems and struggles. However, I'm catching on to the fact that my insights and answers need to take a back seat to being present.

It's been quite a discovery to learn that what helps a person's struggle is not my toolbox of experience and quick fixes. It's simply my willingness to "be there."

Making authentic connections will require intention and vulnerability. When I let my own healing from brokenness and shame guide my response to someone in struggle, this makes me the perfect candidate for participating in the next kind of repair.

PART 3: CALLED

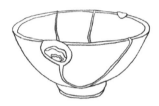

REPAIR TYPE 3: YOBITSUGI – CALL

During my time living in Asia, I had the seemingly monumental task of learning a rather difficult language. The struggle was a day-in-day-out kind of struggle. I once described it to someone as climbing a steep mountain in slick-soled shoes. My saving grace was my tutor with whom I met twice a week for an hour. During one of our sessions, I said something that made her jump back from the table and nearly slide down in the booth laughing hysterically. Once she composed herself, she commented, "Angie! You're so cute!" In that instant, a void I didn't know existed was filled with her words.

To my recollection, no one had ever called me cute. I'm not saying it didn't happen; I just don't remember it. The shock on my face at her choice of words must have been apparent, because I remember having to explain what was going through my mind to her. She was incredulous! And it wasn't the last time she called me cute when something I said or did hit her just right. In those moments of friendship and connection, God placed her in my life and fused us together. To this day, she beautifies me with her kind words and generous spirit. When you see me, she's part of what you see; her unique design is blended with mine.

This particular type of repair is probably one of my favorites. It *calls* for a larger void to be patched with a piece of similar size and shape from a different piece of pottery that was also broken. The other two types of repair may also be used, but *yobitsugi* incorporates an additional element of eclectic beauty.

When I answer the *call* of God to be His, when I am *called* on to share my testimony of how God has worked in my life, or when I simply show an act of kindness, I have the potential to beautify someone else who is in struggle. I also have the capacity to incorporate the beauty of someone else into my life when they share their stories with me and use their gifts to bless me.

I have a wonderful job. I love it! It was uniquely designed just for me at just the right time in my life. As part of this amazing job, I spend about three weeks each year training young people in a short-term missions program overseas. Usually, things go very smoothly, but even without any major snags, it's a stressful time for me as I deal with on-site details, logistics, and team dynamics. As my personality type strives for peace and harmony, it can be a challenge not to be affected by little conflicts here and there that may arise while on location.

For me, God has graciously provided someone who uses her giftings and natural abilities to help keep things running smoothly. When I get tossed a curve ball, she's right there to assure me it will all work out. She's incredible at rolling with the punches. She handles the challenges that would bog me down and wear me out with grace, efficiency, and a smile. During that time, for me to be the best me I can be, it really helps to have her in my life. God has done a *yobitsugi* on us. She beautifies my life administratively and quite literally by turning my frowns upside down. I'm so glad for people like this in my life. I work with them. I go to church with them. I teach with them. I learn from them. When you see me, they are also part of what you see.

If I were to describe myself in light of this idea, I imagine I look like a pottery version of a patch quilt; so many incredible people have answered my conscious and unconscious calls for help. The parts of them they've left behind strengthen and beautify me.

When Titus received his letter from his mentor, Paul, I can imagine him tearing it open. Those two seemed to have quite a relationship! Paul lovingly called him a true son in the faith.[26] By chapter two, Paul is encouraging Titus to promote the kind of living that reflects good teaching. As an aside, I like the idea of developing disciples, but I get excited about the idea of nurturing sons and daughters in the faith. Perhaps this is one of the perks of being single.

One of the concepts Paul gets to in verses 9-10 of chapter two has to do with something called "adorning the doctrine." It sounds fancy, but basically Paul explains to Titus that when the slaves in his congregation obeyed their masters, did their best, didn't steal or talk back, and showed themselves trustworthy in their difficult circumstance, it made the teaching about God attractive in every way.[27] Similarly today, when we honor each other, we too adorn the doctrine. When we treat each other courageously with love, generosity, compassion, and respect, we make our life in Christ extremely attractive to others.

I am so grateful for how God puts people in my path, and when our paths diverge, they leave me in better shape than they found me.

What an incredible Bride of Christ we are becoming together. As we add beauty to one another with testimonies of our stories, shared wisdom, kind words and deeds, as well as truth spoken in love, we are beautifying none other than the Bride of Christ. That's who we are collectively. If you need something good to think on, this is one of those things.

We beautify one another when we answer God's call to share parts of our story with those He leads us to. Let me never forget the testimony of my brokenness and how the expression of my love and care has the power help fill a void in someone else.

HIS POWER THROUGH MY WEAKNESS

The apostle Paul gave us an incredible window to his soul concerning how God's power works through, and in spite of, our weakness. In 2 Corinthians 12:9, Paul hits three major points that I've found to be a refreshing perspective.

He says first that God's grace is all I need. I may not get the grace I need from others, but the grace I need the most is guaranteed. This is revolutionary to me because sometimes I don't even have grace for myself. I get frustrated (a.k.a. angry) at my limitations and struggles, and I just want to pull back into a corner until I can bring myself together. But Paul says, God's grace is the juice I need to keep going. This enables me to inch forward in the face of adversity or to ignore that little voice in my head talking smack.

Paul also assures us that God's power works best in weakness. I've tested it out, and basically, "that man don't lie."

One of the struggles—okay, a weakness—of an Enneagram nine personality type (that's me) is that I don't always believe what I have to say is of any importance or value. There are reasons I default to this; past experiences confirm it's true. However, it's in this weakness, God's power is enabling me to type the content of this book. Could someone else say it better? Most assuredly. But for now, it's up to me. He is showing up where I have a serious lack and is

51

making me strong enough to finish what we've started. His power at this very second is working through my weakness, one word, one letter at a time. Tap. Tap. Tap. My weakness. His power. Tappity-Tap. My need. His grace. Tap.

And finally, Paul declares he would boast of his weakness so God's power could work through him. In other words, he didn't have to hide his struggle. His vulnerability and authenticity allowed God to be clearly on display. That's partly what the previous paragraph is about. I want you to experience hope and trust in God as you read my thoughts on how He can take our brokenness and make it beautiful.

One of the interesting side effects of *kintsugi* is that the repaired joints are stronger for having been repaired. It is said they don't break again in the same places. When His power meets my weakness and engulfs it, I morph. I become a stronger version of myself, surer, because of Him, His power through my weakness. When I am weak, it is then I am strong.[28] Strong I am, when I am weak. Yoda would be proud.

PART 4: TOGETHER FOREVER

SAFE

It was early morning. I woke up to the thudding sounds of "toog toog" and thought someone was banging on the front door. I couldn't figure out why no one had answered the door as the thudding continued. Next, there was a soft tap on my bedroom door and my mom entered to let me know there was a "situation" developing down the road in Manila.

Rebels were attacking Malacañang Palace where the newly installed female president lived. They were also planning to attack Camp Aguinaldo, a military base which was a few miles away from our condo in Green Hills. Those "toog-toogs" were the sounds of heavy artillery.

It was exciting times in the mid 1980's in the Philippines.

Throughout the day, the thudding continued. Helicopter gunships buzzed lazily around the area. After listening to reports on the radio for what seemed like hours, my brother and I escaped to the roof through a window in his bedroom to get a better view. About the time we were ready to go in, our ears picked up a new sound in the sky. And then we saw it. A World War II era, Japanese Toro-Toro plane was lumbering toward our position.

We stood transfixed as the plane slowly rumbled in the sky like a heavy bumble bee. As it neared the military base, it suddenly dropped from the sky in what we expected might be a kamikaze death dive. Amid the sound of the downward whine of its engines, the whistle of falling ordinances and the booms of their explosions sent us scurrying back into the house.

However, despite the commotion around us, we were safe. We didn't really feel it, but we were.

In the newspaper the next day, I got a kick out of seeing President Corazon Aquino in a big picture just above the fold. She was holding up the bed skirt of her bed, showing her bed frame was solid to the floor. She wasn't about to let the media get away with their false claims that she had cowered under her bed in fear as Manila was being attacked.

I started thinking about the difference between *being* safe and *feeling* safe.

The next chance I got, while at the nearby Bible school, I asked a few students, "Would you rather *be* safe or *feel* safe?" The resulting lively discussion split the group, fifty-fifty. I was surprised to find about half would rather feel safe, even if they really weren't.

For me, even though I would like to *feel* safe, I would rather *be* safe. I can deal with the tension between knowing and feeling if I'm sure what I know is accurate.

I bring this up because when we think about forever, we must *know* that it's there in Jesus. He is where our assurance of safety lies. In this world, however, we are often caught in the conundrum of wanting to *feel* it now.

It doesn't *feel* safe to be a Christian in a hostile environment. It doesn't *feel* safe to love with no guarantee of it being returned. It doesn't *feel* safe to step out in faith, to do the hard things we are asked to do. When God is truly in control (which means I am not), it doesn't quite square with my desire to feel safe in this world. Perhaps it can be said that a Christian's version of "safe" is faith. Safe in Him.

When we read about the Jesus of the Bible, we are reminded that He doesn't seem to put a high value on feeling or being safe in this world. Even today, He calls us to serve in unsafe places, in unsafe times, and among unsafe people. Who is "us"? I think you know.

In an effort to generate that feeling of safety, some have flat-out ignored their call to service. Others have answered but cushioned their every response. When they wrap up to protect themselves from a fall, like the kid with all the pillows learning to skate, they limit their mobility, and their commit*ment* easily becomes what they meant to do.

But there are those (perhaps you?) who would rather *be* safe in Jesus, following wherever He leads. In light of eternity, they can handle the discomfort of not always feeling safe. They trust what they know of Him over their feelings. They know from their head to their toes that as long as they're together—them in Jesus, Him in them—they will be safe. No matter what's going on around them, they know there's a better day coming.

And when they break in service they know in their soul: it's not the end of the world.

TOGETHER

There is coming a day when I will no longer be fragile. No longer will I need armor to be strong. I won't have to face my fear of disconnection anymore because I will finally be "together," and as a bonus, I will finally have it all "together!" Look for me; I'll be the one swinging from the chandeliers fearless in the face of a potential fall! This day is the one I'm waiting for because I'll be united with God beyond the confines of my mortal body. Finally, whole! Whole in health, whole in body, whole in spirit, whole in emotions, whole in mind. Whole! Because of Him! He's held me together in this world that I may be whole in the next. And in that condition, I will see His face.

This world is not my home. No matter how much I may feel at home here, this is not the end. I live for the glory of God, not for the glory of this world. And when I feel awkward and out of place, which is most of the time, I must remember "together" is coming. And while I wait for that day, I can enjoy togetherness with others, who like me, have "forever" running through our veins. We may not clearly see who we are becoming, but we know God is at work, putting us together individually and collectively in a way that makes Him shine as light among the nations.

This message, this great news, isn't just for me and you; it's for everyone! Eternity has been knit into every human heart, but many have never heard that there is hope for their broken spirit. They lay broken without knowing of the remedy prepared for them since before their existence. They are strangers to the Master Potter. In truth, my existence as someone who has been repaired by the Master Potter is to allow His story to intersect with mine in a way that gives someone else hope. My continual prayer is, "Jesus shine through me so that I don't arrive there alone." I want to arrive together, having brought others with me.

Yet God has made everything beautiful for its own time. He has planted eternity in the human heart, but even so, people cannot see the whole scope of God's work from beginning to end (Ecclesiastes 3:11, NLT).

I'll never forget the way she stepped to the keyboard, adjusted a few knobs, and pulled the mic into position. She was in pain, but she flashed one of her brilliant smiles to the audience. She breathed in and exploded into a chorus that hit us like a thousand bolts of lightning, uniting heaven and earth. That song shot through the crowd, in an instant making us one as she belted out:

All I know is I'm not home yet
This is not where I belong
Take this world and give me Jesus
This is not where I belong.[29]

And with energy not previously in the room, we belted it out with her. As she played, we danced, temporarily lifted from any present pain and care to a place of wholeness and timelessness. I am as convinced now as I have ever been that I was made for eternity. And that little moment of reprieve is proof to me eternity exists, and I belong there. Have you ever felt that way? Lifted? You belong there too, my friend.

FOREVER

Thinking about forever, in my opinion, is a great mental and spiritual exercise. It can nearly break my brain, but I love thinking about the possibilities that are coming. I ask questions like: "How is what I'm going through preparing me for my role in eternity? How is this decision leading me closer to a 'well done' by my Creator? Is my present distress a test of loyalty and endurance? Am I using all the things God has given me in a way that brings Him glory?" In addition to these questions, I allow my mind to wander, freeing it to extrapolate what kind of things I'll do as an immortal. This has a restorative effect on my soul.

If it's been a while since you've soaked in the truth that forever isn't as far away as you might sometimes imagine, do yourself a favor. Take some time to let it captivate you. Think about these things and perhaps add to the list below a few of your own.

- Time is no longer an issue. There is time for everything. And the space-time continuum is no longer a barrier.
- I will wear a new body, still recognized as me.
- Though Jesus is my ultimate reward, there will be rewards for the quality of my work.
- My little head will wear a victor's crown that actually fits.
- No more bad news. No more waiting for the other shoe to drop. No more tears.
- Sin is eradicated and so is the very temptation to sin.
- I will be able to once again catch up with loved ones and friends who have gone before me.
- My wait to hear the stories and behind-the-scenes details of saints first-hand will be over.

- I will finally get to see Jesus face to face, and mine will most likely be held in His hand.
- Zooming around the universe is allowed... theoretically.
- I will be at one with God and feeling it to my core. No more separation.

I don't know about you, but I feel as though I've been washed by the Word, being further prepared for service. May you and I let our true selves be known, living wholeheartedly here until it's time to move up there. And in our authenticity and vulnerability, may He shine brighter than ever wherever we go and through whatever capacity we serve. We exist to bring Him glory, pointing others to Him.

Together forever. Finally, whole in Him and not alone, bringing others we've influenced with us.

In our weaknesses, through our brokenness, He is strong.

We exist to bring Him glory from now until there is no more *until*.

ACKNOWLEDGEMENTS

"Help my will to crumble," you said. "Whatever it takes," you said. Dad and mom, thank you for setting up our family for a *kintsugi* life in Christ. And thank you for demonstrating what it means to give ourselves away to the glory of God. Answering your call has added beauty to so many broken lives. *Mahal na mahal kita!*

Special thanks to Donna Linville who challenged me to write my first booklet in 2005 and to all those at ECWC 2006 who purchased it! Your belief in me has most certainly added beauty to my life.

When I first debuted this material during a New Life Fellowship Ladies Meeting in Hong Kong, I received such a warm response from the crowd and fellow presenters, that I was spurred on to complete this project without delay. Thank you, New Life Fellowship, for getting excited with me, and for confirming I was onto something! Thank you, Sherie O'Donnell for your encouragement and great advice. *We* did it! *We* really do beautify each other!

For the squad who read the REVISED, REVISED-REVISED, and the REVISED-REVISED-REVISED versions of this manuscript, I bless you! I don't deserve you, but I am so grateful for you all!

To Melinda Poitras, favorite wordsmith of mine (whom I "once upon a time" took to a Build-A-Bear), thank you for your brilliant choice of words in your feedback email; I have played them over and over in my head like a broken record, but in a good way.

For the one who read through the early version of this manuscript as part of his daily devotions, thanks for your thought-provoking and valued feedback. Jim Poitras, plunk, plunk go the marbles into the marble jar.

To all my family and friends who at one time or another said, "It's going to be okay. Everything will work out," aren't you glad it did?

And finally, to the Eternal One, the Heavenly Potter of all, who is over all, in all, and living through all, thank You for revealing yet another side of Yourself to me. The more I know You, the more I love You. The greatest part of me is You! Shine on!

SMALL GROUP ADAPTATION

Below is an outline for how this book could be used during a small group study on brokenness. I encourage you to leave as much room as possible for others to share their stories and experiences in a *safe* community environment.

WEEK 1: BROKENNESS

God uses the broken of this world to bring Him glory. As we surrender to the Him, the Master Potter, healing and wholeness is possible as He repairs us with His Holy Spirit. When we are broken, no matter how it happened, we must stay in the process by keeping hope alive and giving God all the pieces.

Discussion Questions

1. How has your thinking about imperfections in your life been challenged?
2. Describe a recent incident where someone handled you carelessly. How would you describe your response?
3. Describe what surrender looks and feels like in your life.

WEEK 2: REPAIR TYPES 1 & 2 (FILLED)

When we are filled with the Holy Spirit, God begins to fill in the cracks and gaps in our lives. His Spirit joins with our spirit, making us joint-heirs with Christ. As those bigger gaps are filled, we must intentionally keep an eye out for the corrosive effects of bitterness, taking the necessary steps to eradicate it from our lives.

Discussion Questions

1. How do you respond to life when you are filled with the Holy Spirit?
2. Explain the difference between an emphasis on *being* rather than *doing*.
3. What situations tend to lead to bitterness for you and how do you go about eradicating it?

WEEK 3: REPAIR TYPE 3 (CALLED)

As Spirit-filled believers, we have the potential to beautify the very Bride of Christ. When we answer the call—that tug of God in our life—to interact with others in love, we "adorn the doctrine." We can make the Gospel of the kingdom attractive to others in our sphere of influence, no matter where we are.

Discussion Questions

1. How does sharing testimonies of your weaknesses, within your boundaries, strengthen others?
2. Describe how God has put someone into your life to make you a better, or stronger, person.
3. Explain in your own words one key point Paul made in 2 Corinthians 12:9.

WEEK 4: TOGETHER FOREVER

In addition to knowing we are safe in Jesus, we have promises that God has made everything beautiful in its own time, and that He has placed eternity in our hearts. Thinking on these promises is a healthy exercise for our faith. Knowing we can arrive there completely whole, bringing others with us, is cause for celebration.

Discussion Questions

1. In light of eternity, how has your idea about "safe" been expanded or confirmed?
2. When you let your mind wander about eternity, what's the thought you enjoy thinking the most?
3. How would you explain "together forever" in your own words?

END NOTES

Part One: Brokenness

[1] 2 Corinthians 4:7, NLT
[2] Romans 8:38-39
[3] Galatians 6:4-5
[4] Psalm 34:18
[5] Ezekiel 36:26
[6] 2 Corinthians 12:9-10
[7] Dante Bowe, "Potter and Friend," *Potter and Friend*, Dante Bowe Music, 2017.
[8] Ephesians 2:10
[9] John 7:38
[10] 1 Corinthians 1:27
[11] Isaiah 54:7
[12] Brené Brown, *The Gifts of Imperfection: Let Go of Who You Think You're Supposed to Be and Embrace Who You Are*, (Hazelden Publishing, 2010), 65.
[13] Caroline Leaf, *Switch on Your Brain: The Key to Peak Happiness, Thinking, and Health*, (Baker Books, 2013), 13.
[14] Philippians 1:6
[15] James 1:4
[16] Philippians 4:8
[17] Hebrews 6:19
[18] Psalm 16:11, NIV

Part Two: Filled

[19] 1 John 3:2
[20] Galatians 3:26
[21] Angie Clark, *7 Essentials of Kids Prayer 2.0*, (Amazon publishing, 2012), Loc 340 of 2879.
[22] Romans 8:16-17
[23] Kim Parker and Renee Stepler. Pew Research Center. http://pewrsr.ch/2eYAuZM. Published September 14, 2017. Accessed February 29, 2020.
[24] Psalm 17:15
[25] Psalm 119:137

Part Three: Called

[26] Titus 1:4
[27] Titus 2:9-10
[28] 2 Corinthians 12:10

Part Four: Together

[29] Building 429, *Where I Belong*, https://youtu.be/he32vwlKQPY. Published February 21, 2012. Accessed February 29, 2020.

Made in the USA
Las Vegas, NV
11 June 2023